Beautiful
ALPHABET
APPLIQUÉ

ZENA THORPE

American Quilter's Society
P. O. Box 3290 • Paducah, KY 42002-3290
www.AmericanQuilter.com

Ｄedication

This book is dedicated to my mother. Although she is no longer physically with me, she still looks over my shoulder at every stitch I take and insists on the removal of any work that doesn't meet with her approval. Mother was a loving but exacting taskmaster and didn't waste any praise where it wasn't earned. A job well done was its own reward—a philosophy to which I subscribe.

Located in Paducah, Kentucky, the American Quilter's Society (AQS) is dedicated to promoting the accomplishments of today's quilters. Through its publications and events, AQS strives to honor today's quiltmakers and their work and to inspire future creativity and innovation in quiltmaking.

Executive Book Editor: Andi Milam Reynolds
Graphic Design: Lynda Smith
Cover Design: Michael Buckingham
Quilt Photography: Charles R. Lynch

Additional copies of this book may be ordered from the American Quilter's Society, PO Box 3290, Paducah, KY 42002-3290, or online at www.AmericanQuilter.com.

Text © 2010, Author, Zena Thorpe
Artwork © 2010, American Quilter's Society

Library of Congress Cataloging-in-Publication Data

Thorpe, Zena.
  Illuminated alphabet/ by Zena Thorpe.
    p. cm.
  ISBN
  1.
  TT

American Quilter's Society
P. O. Box 3290 • Paducah, KY 42002-3290
www.AmericanQuilter.com

Contents

Introduction

PAGEANTRY

QUILT ON A GRECIAN URN

I have long been fascinated by the illuminated manuscripts produced by monastic scribes of late antiquity. The oldest surviving manuscripts from Western and Islamic traditions date from the period AD 400–600. The text of the manuscripts usually began with an illuminated (heavily decorated), initial letter of amazing and exquisite detail.

When I made PAGEANTRY I decided that this quilt would be my manuscript in fabric on the ancient art of heraldry and so, just as those ancient scribes did, I began the work with an embellished Gothic letter T.

Next I used embellished letters Z-E-N-A to personalize QUILT ON A GRECIAN URN.

My fascination with embellished letters then led me to making a quilt using all of the letters of the alphabet. The art of quilting still holds for me the essence of its early roots and the idea of creating an alphabet sampler such as our quilting forebears often did appealed to me.

Much of the inspiration for the alphabet letters on ILLUMINATED ALPHABET was drawn from Dover Clip-Art books. I have permission or have purchased the rights from them to create this book.

I have always made my own and my children's clothes, so working at the sewing machine became, well, work. Relaxing with hand sewing is just that—relaxation—so my quilts are all worked almost entirely by hand, including the patterns in this book.

General Directions

FABRIC

It is best when choosing fabric colors for the work to choose a strong contrast between the background and the letter and to use this color solely for the letter so that it stands out against the embellishments.

Being somewhat of a purist I am not impressed by theme fabrics and never buy fabric that is printed to portray a specific element, for instance, rocks. For me the essence of quilting remains what it was to those early pioneer quilters who used up whatever they had on hand; I prefer to delve into my scrap stash to discover something that suggests rocks.

100 percent cotton is recommended for all fabrics, which should be prewashed and checked for color fastness.

Remember to cut a ⅛" allowance for turning the edge under appliqué pieces.

Yardage requirements depend, of course, on the number of letters you plan to make. To replicate ILLUMINATED ALPHABET, cut an 11" background square for each letter and the 4 corner squares (to be trimmed later). This will require 2⅝ yards of 40" fabric.

The sashing and binding together require 4¼ yards of 40" fabric.

The 26 letters took about 1 yard total. The embellishments came from many dozens of small scraps.

NEEDLE and THREAD

I use a #10 straw needle and 100% cotton thread. My preferred brand is Presencia® because it doesn't shred or break as easily as some.

PATTERNS

I suggest that you make a tracing of the designs for your patterns. Place the patterns onto the right side of your fabric to cut out the letters (see "Placement"). My usual turning allowance is ⅛", but when I know that an edge will be covered by another piece I cut a more generous allowance to ensure that it will be adequately concealed.

You could, of course, enlarge the letters to suit yourself. Many of the decorative pieces drawn at the scale of this book are very small and require great accuracy in placement.

When making an appliqué picture it is very important to first study the pattern carefully to determine in which order the elements should be applied. A good way to think of this is to imagine the picture in 3-D and then work from the back of the picture, that is, the item furthest from you, and progress to the item in the forefront of the picture.

It is a good plan to then label the pattern pieces in order of placement. I label 1, 2, 3 and so on or A, B, C. Some of the patterns have been labeled, but others I have left up to your personal preference for construction.

PLACEMENT

The pattern may be traced onto an acetate sheet if that is your preferred method of placement or onto a separate sheet of paper (vellum works well) and then transferred to the background fabric by tracing around the holes cut out of the paper pattern. This is the method I use and which I will explain:

After determining which piece needs to go on first, I very carefully cut out that piece with small embroidery scissors so as to not mutilate the surrounding pattern. I can then place the pattern surround onto the background fabric and draw around the inside of the hole. This now gives me the pattern piece to cut out (allowing turnings of course), and also the exact place to attach it. I appliqué that piece down before moving on to the next element of the design. I can now continue to place the pattern surround onto the background with the holes over the work done to show me exactly where the next piece goes and so on. Of course I end up with an awfully messy pattern surround, but tape holds it together satisfactorily.

When faced with the seemingly impossible task of cutting out and turning the tiny hole in a piece such as that shown in figure 1, I cut out the paper pattern. Then, when placing it on the fabric, I open up the pattern slightly to allow sufficient space for turning as shown. When the piece is placed I ease the fabric back into the correct place and I can carefully turn in the edges thus achieving the impossible. This is why I love appliqué; fabric is very forgiving and will bend and form to my will!!

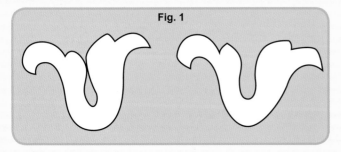

Fig. 1

APPLIQUÉ

I prefer the needle-turn method of appliqué and use a no. 10 straw needle. I find that I have better control using the long needle to stroke under the turning and then hold

the turned section down securely with my thumb as I put in the stitches (fig. 2). However, whatever method works for you is the correct way. As I frequently tell my students, appliqué is an art, not a science.

Don't forget to clip inner curves to just a thread or two short of the stitching line and also trim a little off of any points to reduce the bulk that must be turned under.

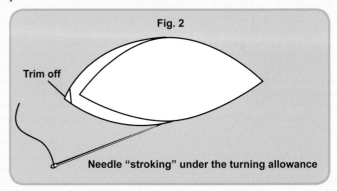

Fig. 2

Trim off

Needle "stroking" under the turning allowance

When pieces join at a sharp angle a smoother line can be achieved by joining the pieces as shown in figure 3.

First stitch B to A without stitching through to the background. Then turn the combined edge in one operation.

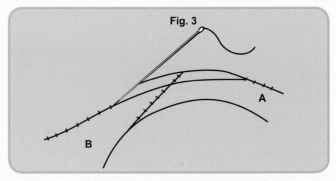

Fig. 3

A

B

Narrow stems are made by placing a ⅜" bias strip along the line drawn for the stem. Make a tiny running stitch a scant ⅛" from the long edge of the strip. When stitching along a convex line, ease the bias strip slightly; when along a concave line, stretch the strip slightly (figure 4). Turn in and whip down the remaining long edge.

This method allows you to make a narrow stem as wiggly as you like, and you can also turn in the end of the stem when necessary. It is best to use a fairly tightly woven fabric for narrow stems; a loose weave fabric could fray.

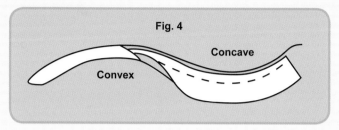

When a stem widens with a flourish at the end, I cut that piece on the bias so that the shape of the flourish is cut correctly but the rest of the strip is a straight piece cut on the bias (figure 5). The flourish can then be appliquéd in position and the rest of the stem is worked according to the narrow stem directions.

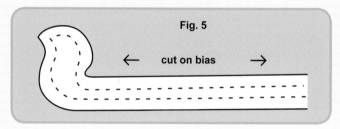

BIAS BINDING

Some of the letters do not have the edges turned in but are bound by a bias binding. To do this, cut ⅜" bias strips as long as possible (to avoid too many joins but not so long that they are unwieldy).

The binding is applied by placing a long edge right along the edge of the letter piece, right sides together, and stitching in a ⅛" seam using very small stitches. Joins may be made by folding in the end of the binding strip by ⅛" and starting another piece by folding in the end similarly and butting it up close.

An inner corner presents no problem; the excess will simply fold in when you turn in and appliqué down. However, when you get to an outer corner you can ensure sufficient material to cover the point by stitching up to ⅛" from the end, backstitch to hold, fold over the strip at an angle and double up to meet the edge just stitched as

shown. As you can see in figure 6, this gives you a little extra and just the right amount of strip to reach the point.

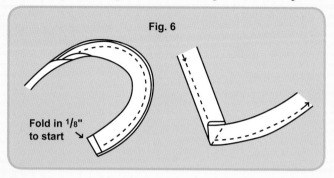

When the strip is applied all the way around, then the binding is flipped over, ⅛" turned under and appliquéd down. This should place the appliqué stitching line exactly on the original cutout line of the letter. It is best to use a fairly close-weave fabric for this to avoid thread breakout.

YO-YO CIRCLES

Draw a neat circle around a bobbin or other article about twice the desired diameter of the finished circle onto the fabric and cut out on that line. A tightly woven fabric works best.

Run a gathering thread of small stitches fairly close to the edge of the circle, but not so close that the stitches break out. Draw up tightly and secure with a backstitch as shown in figure 7.

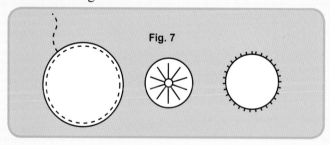

Turn the yo-yo over to the right side, tease into a tidy circle and appliqué down.

YO-YO FLOWERS

Make a yo-yo circle using a 1" diameter fabric circle (a quarter works well to draw around) turn the yo-yo over and bring the needle up through the center of the circle. To create individual petals, take the thread over the edge, bringing the needle up in the center and pull up tightly. Go over once more for security. Take stitches in this manner dividing the circle into 5 evenly spaced petals (figure 8). The yo-yo flower can be stitched into position by going over the petal dividing stitches a third time, but anchoring to the background this time. Work a French knot in the center (see "Embroidery").

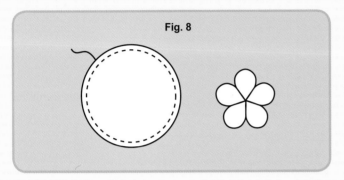

Fig. 8

Very tiny circles cannot be done with this method. For those tiniest ones, I cut a ½", or even less, diameter circle, pin it onto the work and carefully needle-turn it into a neat circle using many stitches to the inch. Of course, if this has you pulling your hair out you can always use beads!

I personalized ILLUMINATED ALPHABET by putting a ladybug on each of the letters Z-E-N-A. If you wish to do the same, or for that matter put a ladybug anywhere on your work, you can make the ladybug as follows:

Make a small yo-yo circle following the directions for small circles but put a little stuffing into the circle before drawing it up. Tease her into a nice shape and appliqué around the edges. The dots and little legs on the ladybug can be added by ink pen or by embroidering with tiny stitches.

EMBROIDERY

For the same reason I don't use theme fabrics, I never use inks for definition work but always use embroidery stitches.

The embroidered details are very important. They add texture and dimension to the work and are often that special touch that brings the picture to life.

Most embroidery is worked with one or two strands of embroidery floss, rarely more. A double line of stem stitch worked finely with one or two strands looks neater than a single line worked with many strands. Keep the stitches small for neatness.

Suggestions for embroidery stitches are given in the directions for each letter.

Stem Stitch
Bring the needle up through the fabric. With the thread to the left of the needle insert the needle a short distance away on the line and bring the needle out again on the line (figure 9). This makes a fine line when using one strand of floss. Two strands will make a slightly heavier line. If an even heavier line is required, work a second row of stem stitch alongside.

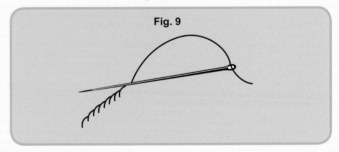

Fig. 9

French Knots
Bring the thread up through the fabric. Wrap the thread around the needle two or three times, depending on the size of the knot required, and insert the needle back into the fabric close to where it came up while holding the wraps closely around the needle (fig. 10).

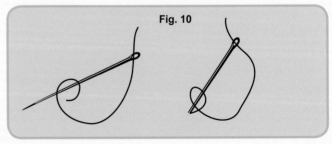

Fig. 10

Flower stamens can be worked using French knots in one operation. Bring the thread up close to the beginning of the stamen, wrap the thread around the needle as with the simple French knot, but insert the needle back into the fabric a distance away as shown while holding the wraps closely around the needle (fig. 11).

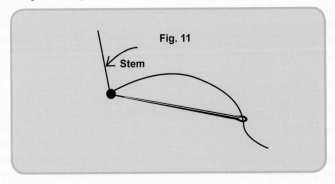

Fig. 11

Stem

Lazy Daisy

This stitch may be worked in a ring to make flower petals. Bring the thread up at the base of the petal, hold the loop with the thumb and anchor it with a small stitch (fig. 12).

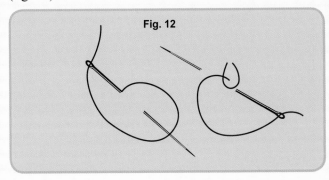

Fig. 12

SASHING

If you are making the whole quilt, be aware that you will need to create the sashing design 71 times and the intersecting circles 42 times!!

O.K., if you are still with me…

You will need to cut 36 vertical pieces of sashing fabric 10" x 4".

The horizontal sashing pieces require 7 strips of fabric cut 66" x 4".

When working the horizontal sections, first mark out the strip starting with ¾" for the binding edge. Then mark a 3¼" section, a 9" section, 3¼", 9" and so on. You should finish up with ¾" at the end for the binding edge again.

These marks will show you where to work the main sections (9") and the intersecting circles (3¼").

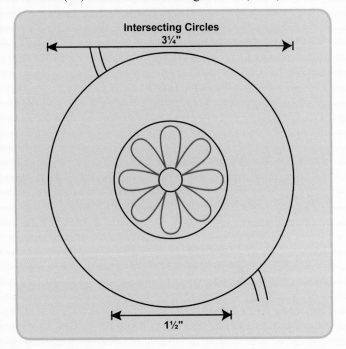

Intersecting Circles
3¼"

1½"

Main Section

The leaves should be worked first—A, then B, then C.

The winding stem is worked following the directions for narrow stems above, but the bias strip should be cut slightly wider at $7/16$". When working the vertical sections you will need to leave a couple of inches extra at each end of the stem to join up with the horizontal sashing.

The gold leaves and small circles are first appliquéd onto a black background fabric, and the shape is cut again from the black a little larger before being applied to the main section.

The tiny stems are worked in stem stitch using one strand of embroidery floss. The spikes around the gold leaves are simple straight stitches worked with one strand of embroidery floss.

Intersecting Circles

Cut the circle exactly on the lines, i.e., no turnings, as the edges will be bound by a bias binding as described above.

The central flowers are eight little petals carefully placed. The entire flower can be worked by taking and repeating a pattern from one of the petals. Cut 8 of them, allowing ⅛" turnings. Stitch the petals right sides together with a ⅛" seam with a couple of securing stitches at the base of the petals. The flower will fall into position, you can needle-turn the rest of the petal, and the untidy center can be covered with a yo-yo circle. Voila!

DIMENSIONAL FLOWERS

The dimensional flowers in letters W and L in the LOVE wallhanging are worked as follows: Cut out the required number of petals, allowing ⅛" for turning, as shown in fig. 13. Stitch the petals right sides together with an ⅛" seam by just a couple of small stitches to secure. Join the first to the last in a circle and then run a gathering thread around the circle at the base. The petals will fall into position and then you can needle-turn the remaining edges of the flower. The untidy center is covered by a yo-yo circle

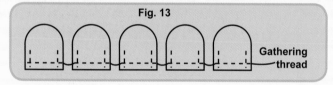

Fig. 13

Gathering thread

FINISHING

Trim the alphabet squares and the corner squares to 8¾".

The border of the squares is now your "wiggle" room. Adjust as necessary to make your square exactly fit the 9" vertical sashing section and join in strips.

As you join in each horizontal sashing section the extra bits of winding stem left on the vertical pieces will be appliquéd in place and slipped under the intersecting circles.

Once the top is complete, layer it with batting and backing. The quilting should not upstage the appliqué.

Bind your quilt, attach a hanging sleeve, and be sure to label your quilt with at least your name and the date completed.

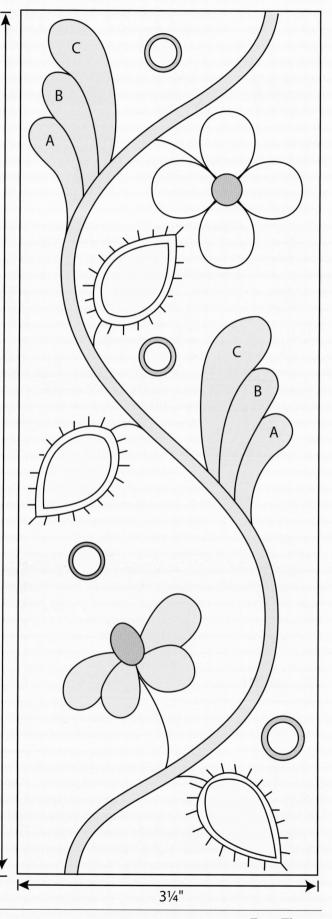

9"

3¼"

Illuminated Alphabet

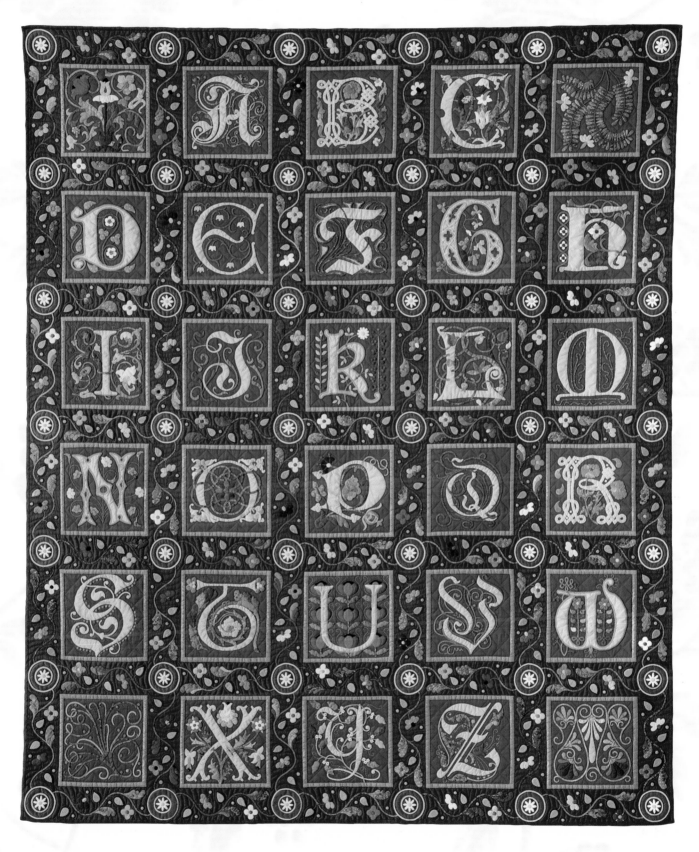

The Letters

This is a very complicated and confusing design. You will find it helpful to first study the pattern carefully and color in the parts of the letter to distinguish them from the rest of the design.

Follow the General Directions on pages 6–7 for appliquéing narrow stems and stems with flourishes.

The bobbles at the ends are most easily worked by making yo-yo circles.

When all of the stem work is done, place the letter pieces in alphabetical order. You can either leave a space in piece C to allow the part D piece to slip underneath or lift a few stitches and then repair.

For this letter you will need to prepare about 2 yards of ¼" bias binding or purchase ready-made bias binding.

Draw the pattern on your background and baste the bias binding in position. You can make any joins underneath a covering strip. Appliqué down, leaving gaps in the stitching where a stem passes under.

You will see that some of the leaves must be placed before the stems can be worked.

Make narrow stems and yo-yos per the General Directions, pages 6–7.

Patterns for all the leaves and flowers can be traced and placed according to the pattern. Where the leaves join at a very sharp angle you can achieve a tidier join by following the directions in "Appliqué" on page 6.

The small dots are made from yo-yo circles.

Please first read the General Directions on pages 6–7 regarding narrow stems, making yo-yos for the bobbles on the letters' decorative ends, and how to separate tightly spaced patterns marked with *.

Study this complicated design carefully to determine the continuing order of placement for all of the pieces. Of course, you can always lift a few stitches to slip a forgotten piece underneath, but it is easiest to get them in the right order in the first place. Trace the shapes to obtain a pattern for each piece.

I cut a slit in the letter to allow the main stem to pass through and then turned in the edges of the slit, but you could simply end the stem on top of the letter to give the appearance of it passing through.

Follow the directions for making narrow stems, bias binding, and yo-yos in the General Directions, pages 6-8.

The narrow stems labeled #1 are worked first, then #2.

The letter may be cut out exactly on the line, i.e., no turning allowances needed since the edges will all be bound with a bias binding. The extra trefoil piece at the letter's bottom left is a separate piece.

Baste the letter securely in place and bind with bias binding. The curl of the letter at the bottom left is simply a continuation of the bias binding applied in the same manner as a narrow stem.

The leaves and flowers may be traced and placed according to the pattern. The flower centers are yo-yo flowers.

See the General Directions for placement.

Following the rule that items behind others must go on first we see that the narrow stems must be stitched first and in the numbered order suggested on the pattern.

If you use the method suggested for narrow stems in the General Directions, which uses a single layer bias strip, you will be able to turn in the ends of the stems. Be careful to leave sufficient allowance at the ends that are to be covered by the next strip.

When the stems are completed you can then applique the center arm of the E, which, if placed carefully, will cover the ends of strips #3 and #7.

The main body of the letter E is placed next and then the decorative ends.

The flowers are placed last and a small French knot is worked in the indentations in the flowers.

As an alternative you can work the stems to the flowers in stem stitch with embroidery floss and use yoyo flowers.

Study the pattern carefully to determine which pieces need to be appliquéd first. You will see that much, but not all, of the decorative scrollwork needs to go on before the letter is worked.

The small pieces of color in the scrollwork are cut exactly on the outer line of the shapes since the edges will be bound by the narrow scrolls. Baste these pieces securely in place before stitching the scrollwork according to the instructions for narrow stems in the General Directions, pages 6–7.

Since there is much passing under and over of the scrollwork in the design, it is necessary to leave gaps in the stitches to allow for items to slip under, or you can lift a few stitches and repair later.

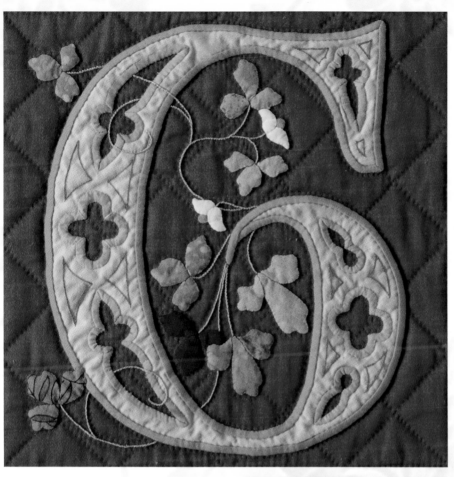

This letter is cut out exactly on the pattern lines, i.e., do not cut turning allowances because the entire piece, including the cutouts, are edged with bias binding.

Baste the letter piece securely in position on the background. Bind all the way around the letter and also around the edges of the cutouts. Refer to the instructions for bias binding in the General Directions on page 7.

The leaves and flowers may then be traced, cut out and appliquéd in place.

The accent lines on the letter are worked in stem stitch using one strand of embroidery floss.

The very narrow stems are worked in stem stitch using two strands of embroidery floss.

Follow the General Directions on pages 6–8 to make the narrow stems and yo-yos for flower centers.

Work the narrow stems labeled #1 first.

Study the pattern carefully to determine the order of placement for ensuing pieces. I suggest #2 and #3 and then section A of the letter.

Continue to study the pattern to determine the sequence of application.

It may be necessary to leave gaps in the stitches when appliquéing piece B of the letter to allow for the narrow stem to slip under in places. Alternatively, you can lift a few stitches and repair later.

French knots are worked around the center of the central flower.

Follow the General Directions on pages 6–8 for narrow stems (except as noted below), tight patterns, and yo-yos.

Appliqué the narrow stems labeled #1 first.

To create the twisted knot at upper right, cut a ⅜" bias strip, turn in one third along one long edge and baste. Turn in the remaining third and baste. The pre-basted stem is then basted in place along the pattern lines and appliquéd down.

There are many places at which you might have to slip a piece under another already stitched down. It is

a simple matter to snip a few stitches and then repair the gap.

Appliqué the letter's shadow after the narrow stems but before the letter body, and the disc shadow in the same pre-basting technique described above.

The tie around the middle is best accomplished by pre-basting the strip into a stem as described for the twisted knot.

The tiny single stems and tendrils are embroidered with a stem stitch, and French knots are worked around the circles.

All of the decorative scrollwork must be completed before applying the letter.

Follow the General Directions on pages 6–8 for narrow stems, stems with flourishes, and yo-yos.

I have given a suggested order of placement but you will need to study the pattern carefully to determine the order in which the pieces need to be applied.

When all of the scrollwork is completed, the letter may be appliquéd in place.

ork the left and right narrow stems first (make them by following the General Directions on pages 6–7, which will also explain bias binding). The ⅜" strip may be cut on the straight grain as the stems are quite straight. Turn in the top of the stem on the right.

Cut out the letter in one piece cutting exactly on the line, i.e., no turning allowance needed, because the edges of the letter will be completely bound by a bias binding. Place the letter and baste it securely in position.

Completely enclose the edges of the letter in bias binding. You can leave gaps in the stitching at places where the central stem goes under the letter or snip a few stitches and repair later.

The central narrow stem is worked next, but the ⅜" strip must be cut on the bias.

Cut 11 petals for the flower using the General Directions on page 10 for intersecting circle flowers.

Appliqué the narrow stems labeled #1 first following the General Directions on pages 6–7.

To appliqué the stems labeled #2, note that there is much weaving in and out of stems. Study the pattern carefully to determine which element needs to be applied in what order. You might have to lift a few stitches here and there to allow a stem to pass

underneath, but these gaps are easily repaired.

The stems which appear to weave in and out through the letter are simply turned in and stop on top of or underneath the letter. They do not actually pass through.

All of the decorative scrollwork must be completed before applying the letter. It is worked following the narrow stem technique described in the General Directions on pages 6–7.

When all of the scrollwork is completed, the letter may be appliquéd in order—A, B, C.

The letter is cut out exactly on the pattern lines, i.e., no turning allowances needed because the entire piece, including the cutouts, are bound with bias binding enclosing the edges.

Baste the letter piece in place.

Cut ⅜" bias strips of fabric in a complementary color. I suggest a slightly darker color for this binding. Cut the strips as long as possible to avoid too many joins but not so long that they are unwieldy. It is best to use a fairly close-weave fabric for the binding strip to avoid thread breakout.

Follow the General Directions on page 7 to apply the bias binding.

Trace the flowers and leaves and appliqué in position. The narrow stems are worked in stem stitch using two strands of embroidery floss. A few French knots trap down and neaten the center of the flowers.

This letter pattern is not for the fainthearted! There are many tiny pieces in the flowers that require great accuracy. For this reason I have included an alternate, somewhat simpler, letter O (in the LOVE wallhanging) on page 60.

Follow the General Directions on pages 6–8 for narrow stems and yo-yos as bobble ends.

The corner flowers must be worked first.

The small stems to the flowers at the top and bottom corners are narrow stems. However, since Celtic knotwork ideally weaves over, under, over, under, this technique just doesn't work for the rest of the knot. These strips need to be pre-basted and then basted in place before appliquéing down. See letter I for directions.

To accentuate the weaving effect, the strips should be two different tones of the same color. Joins may be made under a crossing strip.

I suggest cutting out the letter O and basting it in place initially, because the intricacy of the knot weaves under and over the letter in many places. After all the pieces are in place then they can be appliquéd down.

Appliqué narrow stems first, then letter portion A.

Next comes the curly stem top right and the stem to the central flower followed by pieces 1, 2, and 3, which lead to the central flower stem. The stem leading to the bottom right flower can then be worked.

Next apply the letter portion B and the pointy decorations on the ends. You can achieve a smoother line at the joining of A and B if you first stitch B to

A and then turn in the edge as one. See figure 3 on page 6.

Appliqué the leaf center left before the narrow stem that tops it, then pieces 1, 2, and 3 at bottom left. Follow the General Directions on pages 5–6 for working tight patterns.

The tiny stems to the small circles, top left, (or beads if you are intimidated by such tiny circles), are worked in stem stitch using one strand of embroidery floss.

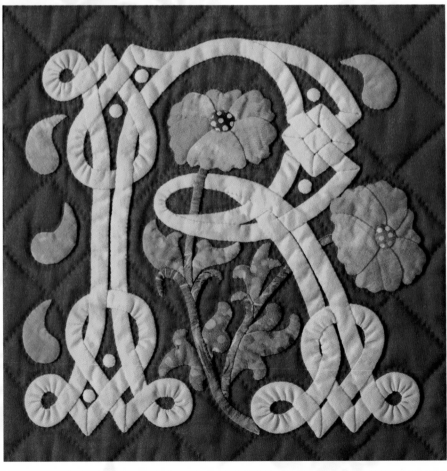

This is a complicated and involved pattern. You might find it helpful to first study the pattern carefully and color in the letter pieces.

Follow the General Directions for narrow stems on pages 6–7.

The narrow stems weave in and out around the letter in a complex fashion, but you can see that the stems labeled # 1 and then # 2 should be applied in order, followed by letter pieces A, B, and C. You will have to lift a few stitches in C for the stem top left to slip under and around.

ake narrow stems, bias binding, and yo-yo circles following the General Directions on pages 6–8.

For this letter you will need to prepare about 2 yards of ¼" bias binding or purchase ready-made bias binding.

Draw the pattern on your background and baste the bias binding in place. You can make any joins underneath a covering strip. Appliqué the bias strips leaving gaps in the stitching where a stem passes underneath.

You will see that some of the leaves must be placed before the stems can be worked.

Patterns for the leaves and flowers can be traced from the pattern and placed accordingly.

Follow the General Directions on pages 6–8 for narrow stems, stems with flourishes, and yo-yo circles.

The narrow stem decorative scrollwork should be completed before applying the letter.

I have given a suggested order of placement, but you will need to study the pattern carefully to determine the order in which pieces need be applied.

When all of the scrollwork is completed the letter can be appliquéd in place.

This is not an easy project! You should study the pattern carefully to determine the order of placement of the pieces.

The letter part A is appliquéd first, however, there are places where the coiling stems go under the letter. I find it best to complete the appliqué and then lift a few stitches as necessary to slip the stem under and repair later.

Work the decorative ends top right and top left. Then part B of the letter can be placed.

The central flower is worked next, followed by the narrow stem leading to it (see the General Directions, pages 6–7).

The flourishes at the top are worked in stem stitch using one strand of embroidery floss.

Poppy stems must be appliquéd first, following the General Directions on pages 6–7 for narrow stems. The fabric may be cut on the straight grain as the stems in this pattern are straight. Some of the poppies and the leaves must then be placed before you can start on the letter. You can trace these from the patterns.

Work the shadowing for the letter in a slightly darker fabric but in the same tones as the letter. Cut a ⅜" bias strip and turn in ⅛" on the long edge. Appliqué this piece along the line drawn for the shadow. The other edge will be covered by the letter which is applied in one piece.

Embroider the tendrils using a stem stitch and one strand of embroidery floss. Keep the stitches tiny to maintain the delicate appearance of the tendrils. The black seeds are worked with French knots using one strand of embroidery floss, or you could use tiny beads.

Follow the General Directions on pages 6–8 for narrow stems, stems with flourishes, and yo-yo circles.

The narrow stem decorative scrollwork should be completed before applying the letter.

I have given a suggested order of placement, but you will need to study the pattern carefully to determine the order in which pieces need be applied.

When all of the scrollwork is completed the letter can be appliquéd in place.

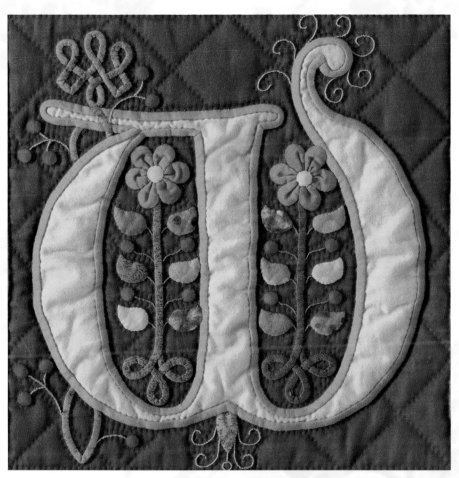

First work the stem at bottom left following the technique for narrow stems described in General Directions. The decorative swirl at top left can also be worked the same way but cannot be completed until the letter is finished. Place the point at bottom center.

Cut out the letter in one piece exactly on the lines, i.e., no turning allowed, because it will be completely bound by bias binding. Baste the letter securely in place and bind around all edges following the directions for bias binding in General Directions.

Work the flower stems as narrow stems, the flowers in six petals as intersecting circle flowers, and the berries as yo-yos. Embroider berry stems and tendrils with one strand of floss.

Follow the General Directions on pges 6–8 for narrow stems and yo-yo circles.

Study the pattern carefully to determine which piece needs to go on first. You will see that some of the leaves must go on before the stems can be worked.

The leaves and flowers can all be traced from the pattern and placed accordingly.

You can either cut slits in the letter as I have done to allow the stems to pass through and then carefully turn the edges of the slits, or place the stems on top of and behind the letter to give the effect of passing through.

First study the pattern carefully to determine the order of application of the pieces.

Follow the General Directions on pages 6–7 to work the narrow stems labeled #1 followed by stem #2.

The letter piece C may be cut out with the long tail at the bottom continued in a straight line on the bias and then applied in the same way as a narrow stem.

The leaf pattern may be traced from the pattern and repeated.

Scatter yo-yo flowers around as desired.

The delicate tendrils are worked in stem stitch using one strand of embroidery floss.

Study the pattern carefully to determine the order in which the elements must be placed.

Follow the General Directions on pages 6–8 for narrow stems and yo-yo circles.

The individual pieces can all be traced from the pattern and placed according to the sequence determined.

The delicate tendrils are worked in stem stitch using one strand of embroidery floss.

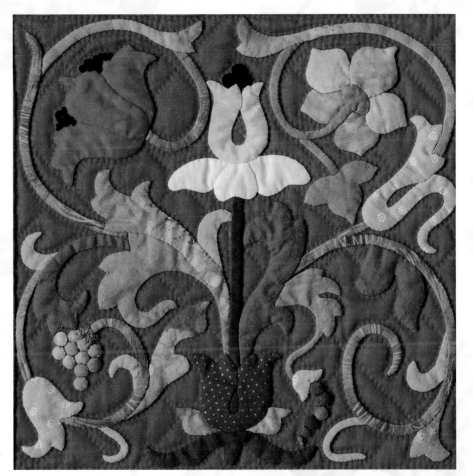

The Corners

Corner Square 1

Follow the General Directions on pages 5–9 for narrow stems, stems with flourishes, narrow openings, yo-yos, embroidery, and placement.

Work the narrow stems labeled # 1 first.

The grapes and other small circles are worked as yo-yo circles.

Work a few lazy daisy stitches atop the bunch of grapes lower left.

Embroider French knots for the seeds in the flower at top left.

Corner Square 2

Follow the General Directions on pages 5–7 for narrow stems and placement.

First work the stems to the flowers. Follow these by the four long stems.

You now get to make a million and a half little leaves. Note the occasional overlapping placement. Happy appliquéing!!

The flowers are worked last.

Corner Square 3

Work the stems following the General Directions on pages 6–7 for narrow stems, but cut the bias strip slightly wider—⁷⁄₁₆".

Study the pattern to determine the order of placement. Stems labeled #1 go on first followed by #2.

The berries are yo-yo circles.

Work the tiny stems to the berries in stem stitch using one strand of embroidery floss.

Corner Square 4

Create the scrollwork following the General Directions on pages 6–7 for narrow stems.

Work scrolls labeled #1 followed by #2. You can then work the long strips.

Trace the shapes for the remaining elements from the pattern. Note that this is a reverse image and you can therefore cut for both sides at once in reverse.

Love Wallhanging

𝔍nstructions for L-O-V-E Wallhanging

Trim the letter squares to 8", join together with ¾" sashing strips in between, and add a border of 1" all around.

*I*nstructions for *L-O-V-E letter L*

The narrow stems labeled #1 are applied followed by stem #2 using the General Directions narrow stem technique on pages 6–7.

The pieces of the letter may be traced from the pattern. They are applied in the suggested order: A, B, C.

Rather than attempt the sharp inner points in B and C, I prefer to place the piece as in figure 14, giving me a nice clean joining.

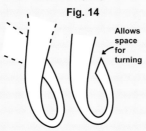

Fig. 14

Allows space for turning

When cutting the fabric, open up the pattern piece slightly to allow space for turning. When you apply the piece the fabric can then be eased back into its correct placement.

Stem #3 can then be applied. You may have to lift a few stitches in the swirl of piece B to allow the stem to slip through.

The flowers are worked as shown in fig. 13 on page 10.

The very narrow stems and delicate tendrils are worked in a stem stitch using two strands of embroidery floss and then the leaves are applied.

Instructions for L-O-V-E letter O

Follow the General Instructions on pages 6–9 for narrow stems, yo-yo circles, and French knot variation.

The narrow stems labeled # 1, # 2, and # 3 should be worked in that order using the technique for narrow stems as described in General Instructions.

The leaves can then be placed in the order suggested: A, B, C, D, E.

The letter O may then be appliquéd in place before completing the stems.

The stamens on the central flower may be worked using a variation of the French knot.

The delicate tendrils are worked in stem stitch using one strand of embroidery floss.

ℐnstructions *for L-O-V-E letter V*

Follow the General Directions on pages 6–7 for narrow stems and widening narrow stems (with flourishes).

The leaf sections labeled A, B, and C, should be applied first.

Work the narrow stems labeled #1, followed by the letter pieces D, E, and F.

The curly stem around F is worked as a narrow stem. You will need to leave gaps in the stitches where the stem passes under when applying F or lift a few stitches and repair later.

Cut 10 petals for the same flower as for intersecting circle flowers. Do not gather.

Work a few French knots around the flower center.

The delicate tendrils are embroidered in stem stitch using one strand of embroidery floss.

Instructions for L-O-V-E letter E

Follow the General Directions on pages 6–8 for narrow stems and yo-yo circles.

The narrow stems must all be worked first in the suggested order 1, 2, 3, etc. Be sure to leave enough at the end of each stem to be covered by a following stem.

Section A of the letter can then be appliquéd covering the ends of stems #6, followed by sections B, then C.

Work a French knot in the center of each yo-yo flower.

The tiny stems to the flowers and the delicate tendrils are embroidered in stem stitch using one strand of embroidery floss.

About the Author

Editor's Note:

ILLUMINATED ALPHABET *won first place in the large appliquéd wall quilts category at the 2008 American Quilter's Society Quilt Show & Contest in Paducah, Kentucky, and 3rd place in the Innovative Appliqué category at the 2009 International Quilt Festival in Houston, Texas. Zena was named one of 30 Distinguished Quilters of the World by Quilter's Newsletter Magazine. In 2003 her quilt* KELLS: MAGNUM OPUS *was designated a Masterpiece Quilt and Zena was inducted into the Master Quilters Guild, an institution of the National Quilting Association. www.zenasquilts.com.*

Zena Thorpe
Photo by John Thorpe

I was born in England and, although I have lived in Southern California for more than half of my life, the ancient history of Britain is a part of my heritage and is thus reflected in my quilts.

In a past life I was a scientist working in biochemistry, but I gave that up for the work of raising four children. However, as was pointed out once by an admirer of my quilts, the technical scientific work, which of course requires great accuracy and attention to detail, probably explains my continued use of that training when making my quilts.

I learned all needle crafts at my mother's knee. Although she was very patient in showing and explaining, what I remember best is the countless hours I spent just watching her work. When the time came for me to try out my own skills, I knew instinctively just how to proceed.

I well remember the night before leaving home on my travels halfway around the world. I needed to get to bed for an early start the next day, but suddenly realized that I needed further instruction on crochet work. Mother got out her crochet hook and gave me one last lesson.

Mother never quilted, so it was after I came to the United States that I learned the joys of quilting. In the beginning I made simple utilitarian Log Cabin quilts for the kids' beds. It wasn't until I became acquainted with pictorial appliqué and discovered that I could create a picture in fabric that I became really "turned on" to quilting.

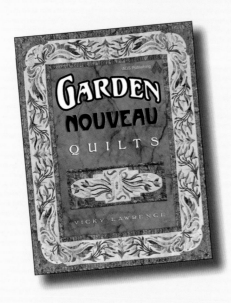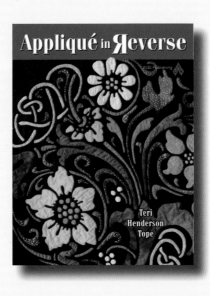
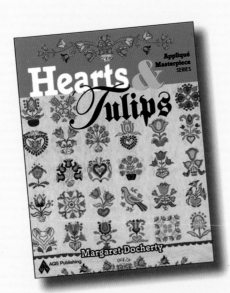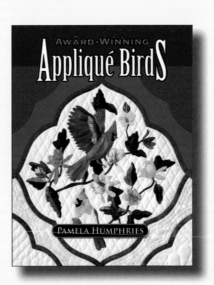